The elegant Angelfish is so
well known that it almost
symbolizes the hobby of
fishkeeping throughout the
world. This peaceful fish
from the waters of the
Amazon is now available in
many different forms.

This book was devised and produced by
Multimedia Publications (UK) Ltd

Editor: Jeff Groman
Design: John Strange
Picture Research: Anne Lyons
Production: Arnon Orbach

Copyright © Multimedia Publications
(UK) Ltd 1984

ISBN 0 8317 8856 9

First published in the United States of
America 1984 by Gallery Books, an imprint of
W. H. Smith Publishers Inc., 112 Madison
Avenue, New York, NY 10016

Originated by D. S. Colour International Ltd,
London.
Printed by Cayfosa, Barcelona, Spain.
Dep. Leg. B - 36.614 - 1984

Tropical FISH

Geoffrey Rogers

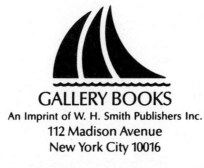

GALLERY BOOKS
An Imprint of W. H. Smith Publishers Inc.
112 Madison Avenue
New York City 10016

CONTENTS

Introduction

Dip your hand into a tropical aquarium and you'll find the water pleasantly warm. This is not surprising since the fishes in the aquarium come from that 'middle band' around our world broadly within the Tropics of Cancer and Capricorn where continual warmth is taken for granted. Spin a globe slowly in your fingers and you'll see that within that band lie the lush jungles and dry grasslands of Africa, the colorful subcontinent of India, the steamy archipelagos of Southeast Asia, the northern reaches of Australia, the sprinkled atolls of Melanesia, Micronesia and Polynesia, and across the vast Pacific to the prolific regions of Central America and northern South America. Add to these land masses the fertile seas that lap their shores, often embroidered with a rich tracery of coral reefs, and you can easily realize that the few fishes contained within a tropical aquarium represent merely a captive drop from a natural reservoir teeming with color and variety.

Choosing tropical fishes

From the vast variety available, which tropical fishes fare best in an aquarium? The easiest to keep are those that live in fresh water – in tropical lakes, rivers and streams. The tiny Neon Tetra from the fertile waters of the Amazon is a popular example of the many active shoaling fishes that bring movement and a sparkle of iridescent color to our private 'windows' on the tropical world. By contrast, many freshwater fishes, such as the curious Catfishes, are sluggish and secretive, becoming active only during the hours of darkness as they search for food at the bottom of the tank. Between these two extremes are

countless freshwater species of various shapes and sizes that will live happily in an aquarium.

Marine fishes, principally those that live among coral reefs, provide a rich source of aquarium subjects. Highly colored, almost gaudy when viewed away from their equally colorful surroundings, the marine fishes demand a more precisely controlled environment than their freshwater counterparts but reward the extra effort involved with a stunning display of exquisite beauty.

Choosing fishes to live together in either a freshwater or marine aquarium demands a certain care; the tranquil waters of a stream or lagoon can hide a bitter conflict. The life-and-death struggle of predator and prey or the capricious jealousy of rival males is intensified in the closed confines of an aquarium and in a short space of time only the fittest will survive.

The fascination of fishes

Fishes were first publicly displayed in glass tanks in London during the 1850s. This created such an interest that scientific collections and more adventurous public displays were set up and these spawned a growing desire among 'fish watchers' to plan a home aquarium of their own. Today millions of people throughout the world proudly call themselves 'aquarists' or more simply 'fishkeepers'. Organized into societies and federations, they are as intense about their fishes as are any truly dedicated hobbyists. The development of a huge commercial trade in tropical fishes has brought the delights of fishkeeping within reach of millions more who are not members of any club but simply share the fascination of fishes, watching through the glass how they move and feed, pair off and reproduce.

The only cloud on such an idyllic horizon is that most tropical fishes are collected from the wild and their quiet streams and sleepy lagoons are not inexhaustible sources of supply. Let's hope that sensible levels of collection from the wild and the successful breeding of more and more species in captivity will enable many future generations of potential fishkeepers to enjoy the simple pleasures a home aquarium can bring.

Opposite Named for its large dorsal fin, this Mexican Sailfin Molly puts on a good show to impress a nearby female. If his courtship is successful, a brood of 30 to 50 live young will be borne by the female after a gestation period of about two months.

3

1 Making Them Feel at Home

The tropical aquarium is literally a life-support system. It must simulate the surface layers of a jungle pool, the leafy margins of a slumbering stream, the sun-drenched shallows of a coral reef. The fishes depend upon its proper functioning in the same way as explorers on the moon depend upon their back-packs. And size for size they may be just as far from home.

Water, light and air

Water is a fish's atmosphere. The fish absorbs oxygen from it and expels carbon dioxide into it through the gills. To keep the water high on oxygen and low on carbon dioxide it needs to be open to the air. That is why aquariums are longer than they are deep so that no part of the water is too far away from the surface. The stream of bubbles that you see rising in most aquariums keeps the water surface turning over to help this exchange of gases to occur.

Most freshwater tropical fishes will live happily in tap water. If you buy them from your local store then they will be quite used to the quality of your local water. Some fishes will thrive only in soft, slightly acid water, while others need especially hard, alkaline water to flourish. These species are generally those that need extra care for success and are not usually recommended for beginners.

A varied selection of aquatic plants can provide a rich backdrop to decorate a home aquarium. Plants also provide essential shelter and spawning sites for many fishes. Try to choose plants with contrasting leaf shapes and colors.

5

Above What a splendid underwater scene this tropical marine aquarium provides! The plants are all forms of seaweed. Among them the flowing tentacles of sea anemones and living corals provide a striking setting for the brightly colored coral reef fishes.

Right A striking marine tropical aquarium in a Dutch home. The brightness of the aquarium lights matches that of the daylight coming through the window – an ideal level for marine tanks.

This freshwater tropical aquarium *far right* forms a superb focal point in the lounge of a Dutch home. Fishkeepers in Holland lead the world in creative 'aquascaping' of their tanks.

Creating and maintaining a 'chunk' of sea water to make marine tropical fishes feel at home is a much more demanding task. Ready-mixed salts are available from aquarium dealers and these should be used strictly in accordance with the instructions.

Lighting the aquarium performs two functions: it shows off the fishes to their best advantage and it simulates the natural light levels the fishes and plants need for normal growth and development. Fluorescent tubes are the most widely used form of lighting and most tanks should be illuminated for about 12 hours a day. Marine tanks are usually more brightly lit to reproduce the conditions of a coral reef.

Some fishes, particularly those that become active during the night, should be kept in fairly low light. If the aquarium contains a mixed population of fishes then floating plants can be used to create dim areas to suit these species.

Right The ingenious use of the space below this freshwater tropical aquarium to grow cacti and succulent plants gives added interest to the whole display.

Live foods are an essential part of most fishes' diet. *Right* Guppies feed on a ball of wriggling Tubifex worms – excellent food for freshwater tropical fishes. Ensure that the worms are rinsed in running water before putting them in the aquarium.

Flake food – available in many 'recipes' to suit different tastes – is an ideal addition to the aquarium menu, especially for surface-feeding species. The Yellow-finned Barbs *below* rise to take some tasty flakes floating at the water surface.

Below right Mosquito larvae suspended from the surface of the water form nutritious live food for freshwater fishes. Here a female Swordtail investigates the larvae as a male waits below.

Warmth, food and shelter

Tropical fishes need to be kept warm; a temperature of 75-81°F (24-27°C) will suit most freshwater and marine species. This can be achieved easily and reliably with modern thermostatically controlled aquarium heaters.

Feeding tropical fishes has also been made easier by modern products. Dried, flaked, granulated, freeze-dried and liquid convenience foods are readily available to suit most fishes at all stages of their development. Live foods, such as worms and small crustaceans, are also an important part of the diet, particularly for marine fishes. Resist the temptation to overfeed.

'Aquascaping' freshwater tropical tanks with gravel, rocks, logs and aquatic plants is not a purely decorative pursuit. Some tropical fishes need the shelter of rocks to establish their own territories and hiding places and all benefit from the oxygen-enriching photosynthesis of living plants. A varied underwater landscape may also play a vital role in the breeding behavior of many species. The marine aquarium is best decorated mainly with inert rocks and coral skeletons on a bed of soft coral sand.

Providing the correct lighting levels is an important part of achieving success with tropical fishes *(above left)*. Here a marine tank is brightly lit to simulate the surface layers of a coral reef lagoon.

The stark rocky terrain of this freshwater aquarium *left* has been set up especially for the African Cichlids it contains. These Cichlids – from the hard waters of the East African Rift Valley lakes – feel at home in these angular, relatively sparse surroundings.

9

Right Light from the fluorescent tubes in the hood of this aquarium combined with daylight from the nearby window keep the many different types of seaweed in this marine tropical tank in splendid health.

Health and cleanliness

Since the tropical aquarium is a living system the natural processes of decay and putrefaction are constantly at work. Waste products from the fishes would quickly poison the water if this was not filtered and partially refreshed with new water every few weeks. Efficient water filtration is especially important in marine aquariums.

In ideal conditions disease is kept at bay, but poor nutrition, low temperatures and bad handling can make tropical fishes more susceptible to infection. Pests and diseases may also be introduced into the aquarium on plants and on new, unquarantined fishes. Fortunately, modern remedies are effective against the most common ailments and are easy to administer. Regular maintenance of equipment and sensible precautions against disease should keep the denizens of our underwater world in radiant health.

Top Low sweeps of foreground vegetation give way to striking outcrops of specimen plants in this well-designed freshwater aquarium. Different levels of planting not only create visual interest but provide territories and hiding-places for mixed communities of aquarium fishes.

These attractive Discus Fishes *left* from the waters of the Amazon River in South America flourish in soft, slightly acid water that is kept very clean. They are best kept in a species tank – that is only with members of their own species.

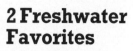

2 Freshwater Favorites

Among the freshwater tropical fishes are many that have become firm favorites throughout the world. These are the fishes that glide and sparkle behind the glass in every aquatic store – the Tetras, Guppies and Angelfishes from South America; the Mollies and Platies from Mexico and Central America; the Gouramies from India; and the Barbs, Danios and Rasboras from Southeast Asia. Some of these have been in demand for home aquariums for over 50 years. What makes them so popular?

The right size

Most of the freshwater favorites grow to about 2-6 in (5-15 cm) in length. This makes them ideal for keeping in aquariums ranging in length from 24 to 36 in (60-90 cm), which is the most popular size range. The Neon Tetra, justly prized for its brilliant blue and red iridescent coloring, matures at just below 2 in (5 cm), and the Angelfish, although usually no longer than 6 in (15 cm), looks appreciably bigger because of its elegant long-rayed fins.

Mature fish size is a vital factor in planning an aquarium because a given volume of water will only support a maximum number of fishes. This is where the area of the water surface becomes an important factor. As a rough guide you should allow 12 square inches (75 square cm) of water surface for each inch (2.5 cm) of fish.

An easy-going nature

One of the thrills of setting up a tropical aquarium is to create a blend of color and movement by mixing different fishes in the same tank. This is easily possible with a wide range of the popular freshwater fishes for they are usually happy to share their living space with completely different species. Ask your local aquatic dealer to suggest a well-balanced collection of fishes including some that swim and feed near the water surface, some that

Left The contrast provided by the elegant Angelfishes and the iridescent blue-and-red Neon Tetras is a popular sight in freshwater aquariums world wide.

swim mainly in the middle water layers and some that feed at the bottom of the tank. Remember to include some rocks and plants that the fishes can adopt as their 'home territories' and all should be well. This is particularly important for the slower solitary species that appreciate an occasional 'refuge' from the disturbing activity of a shoal of fast swimmers. Such refuges are also useful as the fishes in a community collection reach their mature size and start breeding; previously docile individuals can become more aggressive at such times.

Above The more colorful male Dwarf Gourami swims above the female. These peaceful and sociable fishes – excellent for beginners – will thrive even in a relatively small aquarium.

Right First displayed in aquariums in 1906, Harlequin Fishes from Southeast Asia are excellent for beginners. They need plenty of swimming space but also like some densely planted areas which can be used as retreats.

These strikingly marked Penguin Fishes from the Amazon Basin *above* swim in an oblique position in the upper water layers. They grow to a length of 2.4in (6cm) and are long-lived in captivity. Ideal subjects for a mixed community aquarium.

Left The glowing red markings, especially the spot at the base of the tail, give these beautiful fishes the common name of Glowlight Tetras. They are small fishes – only up to 1.6in (4cm) long – but a shoal can sparkle with color and movement.

Available in a bewildering variety of colors and tail shapes, Guppies *above* are perhaps the best-known of all aquarium fishes. They are easy to keep and so prolific that the females may produce live young every four weeks.

Color and variety

Many of the freshwater favorites have been bred into a wide range of 'fancy' varieties that delight the eye. The Guppies and Platies, for example, are available in a bewildering range of colors and tail shapes. The natural variation that exists among these fishes has been extended by aquarist societies throughout the world to produce 'domesticated' forms that do not appear in nature. Such breeding programs not only produce stunning fishes to decorate our aquariums but help to protect the original populations in the wild.

Survival and reproduction

The artificial environment of a tropical aquarium can only be an approximate version of the real thing; the fishes that we boldly release into the water must take their chances. It is to their credit that most survive and even reproduce so far from home. The ability to adapt to their new surroundings is a characteristic of all the 'easy' freshwater favorites. They are hardy rather than delicate. Not only will most adapt to new water conditions but they will also accept processed foods as part of their diet. This is a great boon, especially if you are a beginner to the intricacies of keeping tropical fish. Success with these more accommodating species will give you confidence to try some of the more 'challenging' fishes discussed in the next chapter.

You will find that many of the popular fishes will breed freely, even in a mixed aquarium. Often it is difficult to tell the difference between the sexes, but mating behavior and the appearance of live young or eggs will soon clear up any questions. In the last chapter we explore the fascinating world of fish breeding in more detail.

Platies, naturally bright, have their color greatly enhanced by breeding programs to produce beautiful hybrids like these *above*. Easy to keep and prolific breeders, these popular fishes are ideal for a mixed community tank.

Left These strikingly symmetrical Lyretails – Red female at the top and Tuxedo male below – are a variety of Swordtails. They are lively and sociable fishes and ideal for beginners.

Clown Loaches *overleaf* stay mainly near the bottom of an aquarium, using the sensitive barbels around their mouths to search for live food. Their bold orange and black stripes and long life have made them justifiably popular.

Stylish Black Neons *right* swim over a pebble area that echoes their black and silver coloration. Keep a small shoal of these South American fishes in a tank with some patches of vegetation but which also provides plenty of space for swimming.

The aptly-named Red-eye Tetra *right* will live peacefully with other fishes in a mixed community tank. Be sure to provide some lettuce or other plant food for this fish to nibble and use tough plants to furnish the aquarium – otherwise they will soon begin to look the worse for wear!

How beautifully the Lemon Tetra glows under the right lighting conditions! *Left* The yellow hue of the flank contrasts superbly with the intense red iris around the eye. Quiet and easy to keep, Lemon Tetras reach a length of about 1.6in (4cm).

These dazzling Cardinal Tetras *above* look their best in a dimly lit tank with a dark background. Similar to the Neon Tetras but a little larger, their natural home is in the tributaries of the Orinoco and the Rio Negro in the Amazon Basin.

Far left Two Bleeding Heart Tetras, named for the red marking just behind the gill cover, with a Marbled Hatchetfish. Both species are from South America and can be kept together in the same aquarium.

The intensity of the iridescent colors shining in the Neon Tetra's skin changes with the angle of the light *left.* A shoal of Neons provides a sparkling display in a home aquarium. They are easy fishes to keep and therefore very suitable for beginners.

Above A pair of Black Rubies, attractive fishes that live in the slow-moving streams of Sri Lanka. The rich red of the male shows that he is ready to spawn. Many fishes undergo quite dramatic color changes when they are breeding.

Left Tinfoil Barbs, so called because of their bodies of brilliant silver, are ideal as aquarium fishes when they are fairly small – up to 3.2in (8cm) long. Unfortunately, they rapidly outgrow their welcome, reaching over 14in (35cm) in length. Give them plenty of plant food.

These handsome Giant Danios *above* swim actively in the upper water layers of the aquarium. A secure lid is a good precaution against them jumping out! Despite their name they are not really giants: they grow up to 4.7in (12cm) long in ideal conditions.

Left A pair of the very popular Zebra Danios, the plumper female swimming above the male. These are excellent fishes for beginners, being undemanding and hardy in an aquarium. Like the Giant Danios, they are active and can easily jump out of an uncovered tank.

3 For That Extra Challenge

Keeping some of the 'easier' freshwater tropical fishes successfully can encourage you to accept a challenge. Here we look at some 'difficult' freshwater species that need just that little extra care and attention in the home aquarium. In many cases the aquarium conditions need to be more precisely controlled; some fishes are simply aggressive and unsociable; others just get too large for the average tank. Many of these fishes cannot be mixed with other species in a 'community' aquarium; they must be kept just with others of their own kind. Let's consider the challenge in more detail.

Aquarium conditions

Water quality can be crucial to the well-being of many tropical fishes. The lovely Discus fishes from the Amazon, for example, thrive in soft, slightly acid water, ideally filtered through peat. These conditions can be difficult to maintain without special equipment and frequent monitoring. Other fishes from the Amazon, such as the Hatchetfishes and the South American Leaf-fish, also need soft acid water, as do the beautifully colored Lyretails from West Africa.

The almost circular shape of the Discus from the Amazon River creates a striking impression. There are many color forms of these magnificent fishes, ranging from brown to deep blue and the combination shown *opposite*. These delicate fishes need expert care.

A Silver Hatchetfish swims above a much smaller Marbled Hatchetfish *below*. The Silver Hatchetfish is particularly difficult to keep in an aquarium because it needs a high proportion of live food and prefers to take it at the water surface; if the food sinks the fish may ignore it.

At the other extreme, many species flourish in hard, alkaline water. The classic examples are the Rift Valley Cichlids from East Africa. These unique fishes, many restricted to one lake only, feel quite at home in a relatively spartan tank dominated by rocks. To complicate matters further, several freshwater fishes need sea-salt added to the water! The concentration needed varies from species to species; most of these fishes come from coastal areas where fresh and salt water intermingle.

How the aquarium is furnished with rocks and plants can also make the difference between success and failure with many 'difficult' fishes. This is particularly so with the shy species, such as the unusual Bumblebee Fish from Borneo, which will make good use of any convenient hiding places in the tank.

Top A stunning blue, the male Fuelleborn's Cichlid is an attractive aquarium fish from Lake Malawi.

The Butterflyfish from tropical West Africa *above* can glide for short distances over the surface using its outstretched fins.

The boldly striped Golden Cichlids *opposite* are from Lake Nyasa in East Africa. The darker male is chasing the female in a courtship display.

Voracious predators

Who would not experience a thrill to keep an aquarium full of Piranhas? Their reputation for ferocity may be exaggerated, but they certainly demand respect! Young specimens of the Red Piranha from the Amazon River and its tributaries can be kept in a separate tank furnished with tough plants and filled with soft, slightly acid water. The predatory Pike Characin from tropical West Africa, only 6 in (15 cm) long, also demands a tank of its own. In a community tank it will attack larger fishes. The South American Leaf-fish is also a voracious predator. These predatory fishes are difficult to keep because they need plenty of live food in their aquarium diet if they are to survive.

Many usually docile fishes become aggressive at breeding time and rival males often fight for the favours of a female. The Siamese Fighting Fish is a well-known example; it is possible to keep a male with one or two females but never two males in the same tank.

The sharp, backward-pointing teeth of the carnivorous Piranha from South America *far left* enable a shoal excited by blood in the water to strip the flesh from a large animal in minutes.

The Red Piranha *bottom left* is suitable for a home aquarium only when young and should be fed on worms, insects, fish and meat.

Left The South American Leaf-fish is almost impossible to detect in the water. Unsuspecting fishes investigate the wormlike 'lure' on the predator's lower lip and are engulfed by the large protrusible mouth.

Streamlined Pike Characins *below,* formidable predators in their native West African rivers, like subdued lighting, plenty of vegetation in which to lie in wait, and a varied diet of live insects and fish.

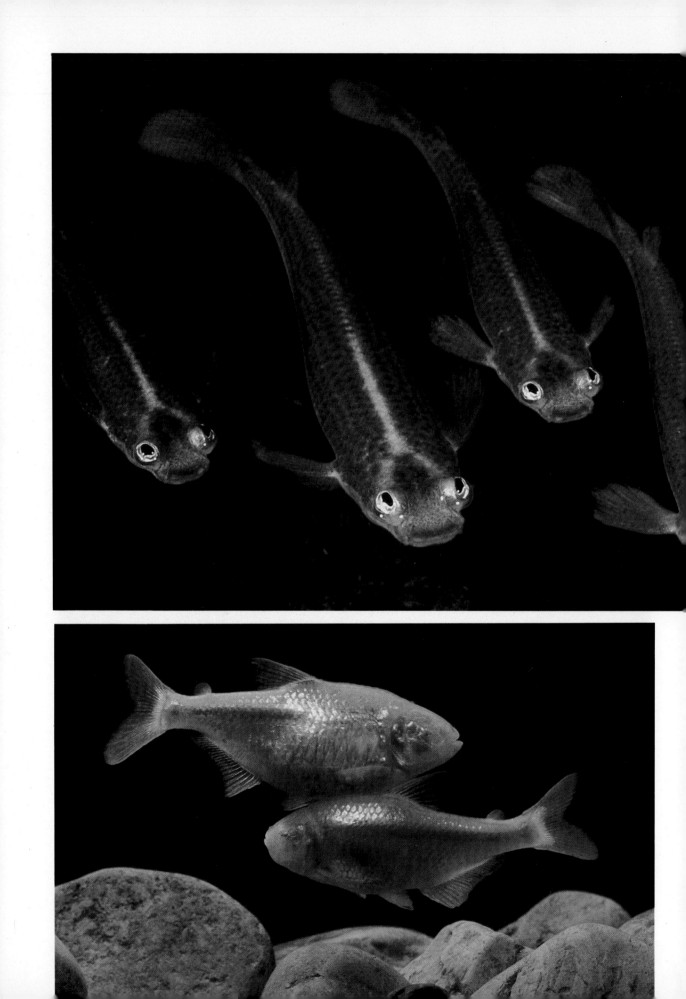

The protruding eyes of these surface-dwelling fishes *left* are divided at the waterline into an upward-looking portion and a downward-looking portion. They can literally look for food below the water and scan the sky for predatory birds at the same time. The common name of Four-eyes aptly describes this unusual arrangement. Keep these curious fishes in a shallow tank with a close-fitting lid: they jump well.

Skin covers the non-functional eyes of these adult Blind Cave Fish from the southern USA and Central America *bottom left*. They can detect food in their natural underground waters by smell and by sensing vibrations. They make a fascinating subject to keep in a specimen tank.

The delicate and the curious

Keeping unusual fishes can be a fascinating challenge. A small shoal of transparent Glass Catfishes from Southeast Asia, for example, make a striking sight in the aquarium. This delicate fish can be mixed with other species of similar size provided there are some hiding places among the aquarium plants. The Blind Cave Fish from Mexico holds a similar fascination.

Fishes with electric organs are of special interest. The Banded Knifefish from Central and South America emits weak electric pulses to navigate in murky water and during its nightly hunt for food. This large fish (up to 24 in/60 cm) should be kept in a spacious tank, but not with other species.

From the same geographical area comes the so-called Four-eyes, a long flattened fish with bifocal eyes that can see clearly above and below water at the same time. In the wild the exposed upper part of the eye registers the approach of predatory birds. This curious fish needs a shallow tank to simulate its coastal water habitat.

The coastal waters of Southeast Asia play host to another surface-dwelling fish that actually obtains some of its food from above the water. The Archerfish can direct a stream of droplets from its mouth to knock unwary insects off overhanging leaves. You can keep this fascinating fish with its own kind in a shallow aquarium furnished with rocks and plants that grow above the surface.

Archerfishes *opposite*, up to 10in (25cm) long in the wild, can be kept in a shallow tank with a rocky terrain and with plants that grow above the water. Provide a varied diet of live foods such as worms and insects; placed on leaves above the surface they will soon be shot down by the deadly accurate Archerfishes.

The beautiful color contrast of the red iris and blue-striped body of the Discus commends this striking fish for the home aquarium *left*. The freshwater Discus thrives in a deep tank containing soft, slightly acid water filtered through peat.

The action photograph *above* catches an Archerfish in the act of 'shooting down' an insect from an overhanging leaf. The triangular snout acts like a bellows as the gill covers close suddenly to force water through the tube formed between the tongue and the roof of the mouth.

A male Mexican Sailfin
Molly shows off his
magnificent dorsal fin in a
courtship display *above*.
These handsome fishes
from southeastern Mexico
can be kept successfully in a
large tank in medium-hard
water with some added sea
salt. Keep a single pair;
males may fight.

Appearances can be deceiving, for these Kissing Gouramies *above* are not 'kissing' at all but testing each other's resolve in a head to head confrontation. Although these fishes can be mixed with other species they are often aggressive to smaller fishes.

The conflict of rival males – a recurrent theme in the natural world – is seen at its most colorful in the Siamese Fighting Fish *left*. Here two males sporting resplendent fins engage in a 'lateral display' of mutual contempt. Keep a male with one or two females but never two males together.

4 The Magnificent Marines

Magnificent is not too grand a word to describe the marine tropical fishes. Those suitable for home aquariums are mainly collected from the world's coral reefs – dazzling communities of color and movement in the upper sunlit waters of the tropical seas. An artist could not conjure up such a rich collection of colors and patterns as displayed by the coral reef fishes. One species, named the Picasso fish, symbolizes the comparison. This fish, also known in Hawaii as *humu-humu-nuku-nuku-a-pua'a*, is daubed with spots and stripes as if each individual had been painted for an underwater exhibition. The coral reef fishes look splendid enough in their natural habitat; when displayed against the more muted background of an aquarium they simply shine!

Some marine tropical fishes can be kept only as juveniles – they either grow too large or become too aggressive as they mature – but many make superb aquarium specimens that fire the enthusiasm of more experienced aquarists. Most marines need a high proportion of live food in their diet, although some, such as the Blacktailed Humbug and White-spot Humbug, will take amounts of freeze-dried and other processed foods. Very few marine tropical fishes can be bred successfully in an aquarium.

Why are the marine tropical fishes so colorful?

Left A coral reef in the Red Sea, alive with brightly colored fishes that shoal in the sunlit surface layers of the warm water. Many of these fishes can be displayed in home aquariums but the conditions must parallel those in nature for success: clean warm water with a constant salt balance, high light levels and a varied diet with many live foods.

This elegant Yellow Seahorse *below,* up to 12in (30cm) long, hardly resembles a fish at all. It uses the prehensile tail to attach itself to seaweed. Feeding in the aquarium is difficult, mainly because seahorses take only small live food.

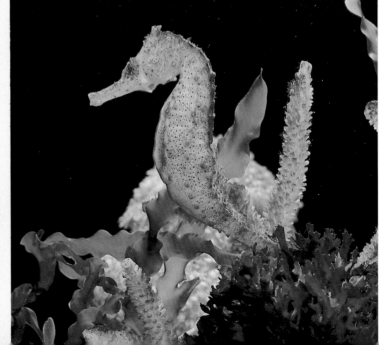

The juvenile form of the Blue Angelfish *above* has quite different markings compared to the adult. It is also known as the Koran Angelfish because the tracery of blue lines near the tail on some juveniles has been interpreted by Moslem fishermen as verses from the Koran written in Arabic script.

The protruding jaw of the adult Blue Angelfish *right* is typical of this family of reef fishes. The mouth contains bristle-like teeth, which are quite adequate for its diet of algae, coral polyps and crustaceans. It reaches a length of about 14in (36cm).

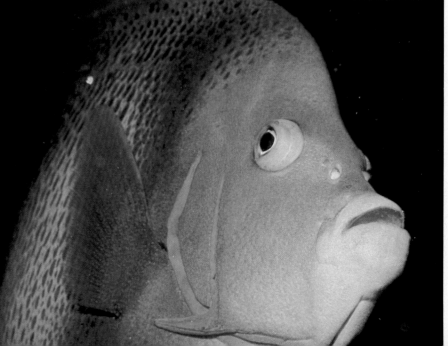

Color to confuse

The vivid color and patterning that we appreciate in the aquarium usually serve a useful purpose in the natural coral reef environment. Many species benefit from 'disruptive coloration' that breaks up the fish's outline against its multicolored background or deliberately misleads a would-be predator to strike at a less vital point – at the tail instead of the head, for example. This is important for those with an almost circular, compressed body shape, for they present a large target. On these fish nature's palette has worked its most intricate designs: spots near the tail lead the aggressor away from the head; bold stripes through the eye help to hide its position.

Above A pair of Pennant Coralfishes. These widely distributed reef fishes are easily confused with the similar Moorish Idol. Keep them in pairs or in a small shoal.

Overleaf A handsome trio of Butterflyfishes, all reflecting the colors and patterns typical of the family. At top right, with the distinctive spot on the dorsal fin, is a Golden Butterflyfish (also known as the Threadfin Coralfish). Following behind is a Chequered or Pearlscale Butterflyfish and below it is a Rainbow Butterflyfish.

41

Fortunately for fishkeepers, these markings are particularly vivid on juvenile fish, those most in need of its protective function and those most suitable for home aquariums. Look for these color schemes on Coralfishes, Butterflyfishes, Angelfishes, Humbugs, Sergeant-majors, Surgeonfishes and Triggerfishes, all of which are candidates for the marine tropical aquarium.

The combination of distinctive markings and curious behavior patterns can make some tropical marine fishes virtually disappear from sight. A striking example of this is the Razorfish or Shrimpfish, an elongated species up to 6 in (15 cm) long that swims head down for much of the time and is often seen between the long spines of sea urchins. The dark stripe along the Razorfish's body and the long dorsal spine projecting from the tail complete its camouflage.

A White-breasted, or Powderblue, Surgeonfish *far left*. These strikingly marked fishes feed mainly on algae and derive their common name from the bony 'scalpels' that can be erected near the tail for use as weapons.

These Razorfishes or Shrimpfishes *bottom left* conceal themselves head down among the spines of sea urchins for protection. Their long thin bodies and projecting dorsal spines complete the effective camouflage. They swim in a vertical, head-down position.

Left Aptly named the Copperbanded Butterflyfish, this beautiful coral reef fish uses its long snout to search out crustaceans and small worms concealed in coral crevices.

The local Australian name for the fish *below*, the Longbill, neatly describes its appearance. It is also known as the Long-snouted Coralfish, and feeds on crustaceans and worms in the same way as the Copperbanded Butterflyfish.

45

Color to advertise and deter

Color and distinctive patterns are not only used to confuse predators. In some cases they draw attention to a 'service' the fish can perform, or warn of a dangerous weapon to avoid. The bold longitudinal stripe on the Cleaner Wrasse, together with its characteristic wriggling swimming action, advertises this small fish as a cleaner and allows it to approach and remove dead skin and parasites from large predatory fish without coming to any harm. This 'uniform' and appeasing behavior has been successfully mimicked by the Sabre-toothed Blenny, which takes the opportunity to bite pieces from unwary 'clients'.

The Mandarin Fish *left* appears to be wearing a cloak of flowing silk printed in a kaleidoscopic pattern of many colors.

The Blue-girdled Angelfish *far left* can be kept in a reasonably large aquarium, where it will feed on Tubifex worms, chopped fish, prawns, brine shrimps and plant food, reaching a length of about 8in (20cm). It is common in the coral reefs of Indonesia, the Philippines and Melanesia.

Known as Lo, Badger Fish or Foxface, these boldly marked fishes *left* graze on algae in shallow waters. They are shy and peaceful fishes in an aquarium but raise their spines when threatened and therefore must be handled with extreme care.

The compact Black-tailed Humbug *left* is an ideal fish to keep in a tropical marine aquarium. It grows to only about 3.2in (8cm) long and will take a wide range of foods, including dried foods. It is a common fish on the Great Barrier Reef near Australia.

The elaborate markings of the Lionfish or Scorpionfish warn of the venom glands that lie within its dorsal spines; one touch and they will inject a powerful nerve toxin. Despite its deadly potential this colorful fish is a popular and adaptable aquarium species.

Left What a splendid show these two Scorpionfishes put on! While admiring their beauty it is as well to remember that those dorsal spines can inject a powerful nerve toxin. They are also known as Lionfishes, Dragonfishes and Turkeyfishes and, despite their powerful armory, they are amenable and popular aquarium fishes.

Many marine tropical fishes, such as this Gaimard's Rainbowfish or Tomato Wrasse *above,* are at their most colorful in the juvenile stage. The adults of this fish are neither so attractive nor really suitable for keeping in an aquarium. This fish wriggles through the water rather than swims and rests on its side on the bottom at night.

Both the Clownfish and the sea anemone shown *above* gain from their close relationship. The fish is able to secrete a mucus covering that matches that of the anemone's tentacles, thus 'fooling' the anemone that the fish is part of its own body. The fish thereby gains a refuge from danger and the anemone has its tentacles cleaned by the foraging action of the fishes.

The Yellow-tailed Clownfish like the one shown *right* is excellent in a home aquarium.

The Clownfish or Anemone-fish *far right* will even lay its eggs at the base of an anemone for safe keeping.

A colorful association
The close association of Clownfishes
and sea anemones not only looks
attractive but also serves a purpose.
The lovely Clownfishes, boldly
marked in orange, black and white,
nestle in the sting-laden tentacles of
large sea anemones, apparently safe
from the anemone's potentially fatal
armory. The fishes secrete a mucus
covering that exactly matches that of
the anemone, which treats the
'intruders' as part of its own body. In
return for providing a sanctuary from
danger, the anemone may have
parasites cleaned from its tentacles by
the Clownfishes. Clownfishes kept in
the aquarium should be accompanied
by a suitable anemone. Such
associations are common in the busy
and varied world of the coral reef.

5 Breeding Tropical Fishes

Some freshwater tropical fishes build a nest and then lay eggs in it. The nest is formed by the male fish at the water's surface; it consists of bubbles and fragments of plants. Bubblenest building is just one of the ways freshwater tropical fishes try to protect their eggs. Many species take less care, while others bear fully formed live young. These breeding activities can be observed and encouraged in the aquarium.

Marine fishes are more difficult to breed in captivity, especially in smaller-size home aquariums. So let's concentrate on the freshwater fishes.

The casual egglayers

For most freshwater tropical fishes kept in aquariums, reproduction is random. The female scatters her eggs and the male fertilizes them as they fall to the bottom. Beginners' fishes such as the Tetras, Barbs and Danios, breed in this free and easy way. To compensate for losses, some fishes produce one thousand or more eggs. In the wild, water currents carry the fertilized eggs away from the parents, which is fortunate because the parents relish eating them! In the aquarium, separate the parents and eggs after spawning.

Responsible parents

The care that tropical fishes give to their eggs and young is geared to the hazards that face them in their natural environments. The Annual Toothcarps, such as the Argentine Pearlfish and the Red Aphyosemion from West Africa, live in small pools that completely dry up sometime during the year. The fishes overcome this interruption of their life cycle by laying eggs in the mud before the pools dry up. These eggs remain dormant until the rains return, perhaps months later. Many of these fishes will bury their eggs in peat provided for them at the bottom of the aquarium, and then die – even though they are in no danger.

Left A male Black Ruby in dark red courtship colors actively pursues a female in a ritual known as 'driving'.

Several fishes guard the eggs for two or three days until they hatch. This behavior is seen in several Cichlids, including Angelfishes, the Firemouth Cichlid and Kribensis. The eggs are laid on a chosen and cleaned rock or leaf, usually guarded by both parents. The Spraying Characin from South America lays eggs on the underside of an overhanging leaf; the male and female repeatedly flip themselves out of the water and spawn, clinging on to the leaf, until hundreds of eggs are stuck to the leaf. The male flicks water over them with his tail until they hatch and the young fall into the water.

Before spawning these male and female Jewel Cichlids from Africa *left* investigate possible sites. Here they clean and try out a flat stone in the aquarium.

The female Jewel Cichlid carefully lays a batch of translucent eggs on the stone as the male hovers close by ready to fertilize them *bottom left*. Since they lay their eggs in the open these Cichlids are known as 'open spawners'; some Cichlids, the so-called 'secretive spawners', lay their eggs in crevices or caves.

Above Fanning water over the eggs is an essential part of the incubation process; both parents take turns. The eggs hatch after about three to five days.

A proud parent escorts a shoal of three-day old fry *left*. Immediately after hatching, the parents transfer the fry to the relative safety of a pre-dug shallow pit in the sand or gravel. Both parents tend the fry until they are at least 0.4in (1cm) in length.

Overleaf Male and female Dwarf Gouramis from Southeast Asia in a courtship display. The male is more colorful than the female, with more fully developed dorsal and anal fins. During this ritual the male moves the female towards the bubblenest.

The bubblenest builders mentioned earlier include many types of Gourami and the Siamese Fighting Fish. Once the eggs are safely installed in the nest the male fish guards them until they are free-swimming. In the aquarium, remove the female once the eggs are laid. The eggs hatch in about 24 hours and the fry stay in the nest for several days more feeding on their yolk-sacs.

A male Dwarf Gourami builds a bubblenest at the water surface in preparation for spawning. The male forces out streams of air bubbles from the gill openings and forms them into a frothy mass, often anchoring it among floating plants. The oxygen-rich nest gives the eggs and fry a good start in the murky waters of their native streams. Gouramis spawning beneath a bubblenest *left* and *below.* The male has turned the female over and has wrapped his body around her to squeeze out the eggs and fertilize them as they float up to the nest. After spawning, the male guards the eggs. They hatch in about 24 hours and the fry stay in the nest for a further five days, feeding on the contents of their yolk-sacs.

Right A male Siamese Fighting Fish making a bubblenest at the surface. This is the first stage in the spawning sequence. As he builds the nest he seems to have no time for the female, but once the nest is ready he is anxious to position her below it for spawning.

Amazing mouthbrooders

Females of the Cichlid group take the fertilized eggs into their mouth and incubate them for about ten days until they hatch. Fishes such as the Egyptian Mouthbrooder and Mozambique Mouthbrooder raise their young in this way. After the eggs hatch the fry stay near the mother for several days, seeking the safety of her mouth when danger threatens.

The carefree egg-scatterers may lay a thousand eggs, but as the degree of parental care increases the number of eggs laid goes down. The mouthbrooders may incubate only a dozen or so eggs in each cycle.

Left The female African Mouthbrooder picks up the newly laid eggs in her mouth. Compared to the thousand or so eggs laid by less 'caring' parents, these mouthbrooding fishes may lay only a dozen eggs. The male fish stays close by.

Far left The female investigates the egg-shaped markings – so-called 'egg dummies' – on the anal fin of the male fish. As she does so the male sheds his sperm to fertilize the eggs in the female's mouth.

Left The female spits out a mouthful of babies she has retrieved from the edge of her territory. The babies stay close to the mother for up to seven days after hatching, retreating into her mouth whenever danger threatens.

61

Fishes that bear live young

The ultimate in parental care –
bearing live, fully-formed young –
occurs in many popular freshwater
tropical fishes. The prolific Guppy can
produce 20 to 100 live young every
four weeks. Other popular livebearers
include the Mollies, Swordtails and
Platies. The females of most of these
fishes can produce several broods
from one mating; the male's
spermatozoa is stored and remains
fertile within the female's body.

Breeding such fishes as Guppies is
no problem for beginners. If you wish
to breed particular color strains of
these very ornamental fish keep the
chosen strains in separate collections;
males will breed prolifically with any
strain and disrupt your plans. Use a
breeding trap so that the newly born
young can escape harassment by the
female fish.

The female Swordtail jerks
away as she ejects live
young *left*. It is best to
transfer a pregnant female
to a separate tank free from
the attentions of the male fish.

Above The female Swordtail giving birth. Her swollen belly clearly shows that there are more on the way. Depending on her size, she will produce between 20 and 200 live young after a gestation period of four to six weeks.

Day-old Swordtail fry swim near the surface in search of food *left*. Special foods in liquid or finely powdered form are available for young fry. In ideal conditions, they will grow rapidly and can be accustomed gradually to taking live and processed foods. Keep the fry-raising tanks fairly dim at first.

PICTURE CREDITS

Biofotos/Heather Angel 14t, 20b, 27b, 45b, 47t **Ardea** 40b, 46t, 50b **Bruce Coleman** back cover, end papers, 1, 2, 8, 12-13, 15, 16, 17, 18-19, 20-21t, 22, 23b, 24r, 25, 26-27, 28t, 29, 30, 31, 32b, 34, 35t, 36, 37, 39b, 40t, 41, 42-43, 44, 45t, 46b, 48-49, 50-51t, 52-53, 54, 55, 56-7, 59, 60, 61, 62, 63 **M. Sandford** 4-5, 7b **Seaphot Limited: Planet Earth Pictures/Warren Williams** 38-39 **W.A. Tomey** 6, 7t, 9, 10-11, 14b, 21b, 23t, 28b, 35b, 51r. **A. Van Nieuwenhuizen** front cover, 24l, 32-33, 47b, 58

Multimedia Publications (UK) Limited have endeavored to observe the legal requirements with regard to the rights of suppliers of photographic material.

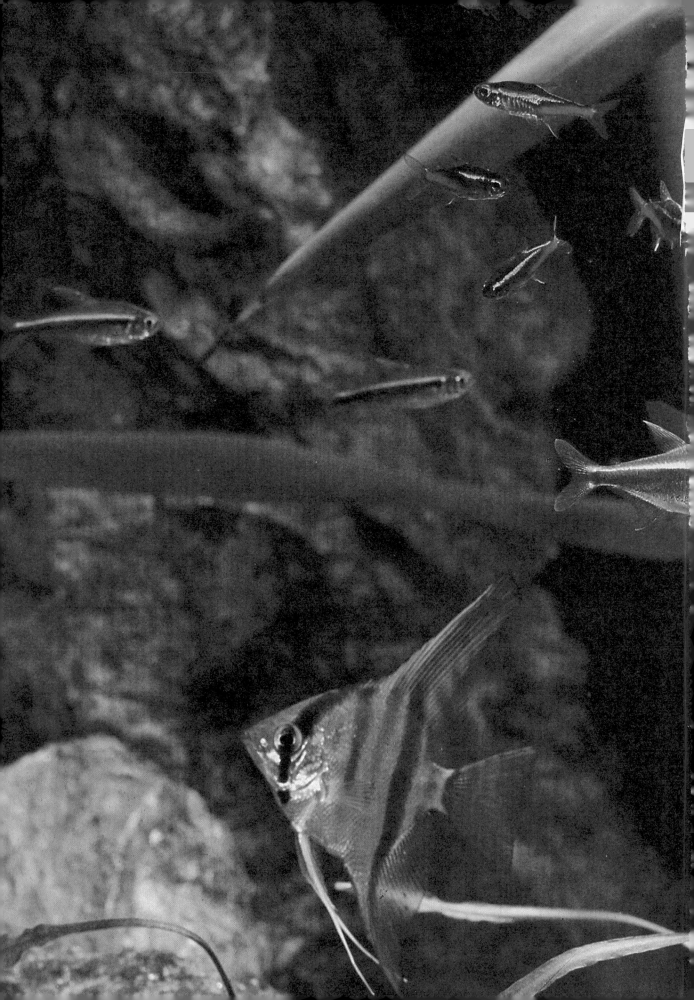